Mini
Early Elementary

A DOZEN A DAY
SONGBOOK

PLAYBACK+
Speed • Pitch • Balance • Loop

Each piece includes two audio tracks: one with piano and orchestration at a practice tempo, and one with just the orchestration at a faster performance tempo. With our exclusive *Playback+* feature, you can change the tempo even more without altering the pitch, plus set loop points for continuous repetition of tricky measures.

To access audio, visit:
www.halleonard.com/mylibrary

3218-1148-6723-5368

ISBN 978-1-4234-7561-3

WILLIS MUSIC

EXCLUSIVELY DISTRIBUTED BY

Hal•Leonard®

Visit Hal Leonard Online at
www.halleonard.com

NOTE TO TEACHERS

This collection of Broadway, movie and pop hits can be used on its own or as supplementary material to the iconic *A Dozen A Day* technique series by Edna Mae Burnam. The pieces have been arranged to progress gradually, applying concepts and patterns from Burnam's technical exercises whenever possible. Teacher accompaniments and suggested guidelines for use with the original series are also provided.

These arrangements are excellent supplements for any method and may also be used for sight-reading practice for more advanced students.

CONTENTS

Love Me Tender

Use with A Dozen a Day Mini Book,
after Group I (page 8).

Words and Music by Elvis Presley
and Vera Matson
Arranged by Carolyn Miller

Warmly

Love me ten - der, love me sweet; nev - er let me go.
You have made my life com - plete, and I love you so.

Love me ten - der, love me true, all my dreams ful - fill.

For, my dar - lin', I love you, and I al - ways will.

Accompaniment (Student plays one octave higher than written.)

Warmly

With pedal

Lean on Me

Use after Group I (page 8).

Words and Music by Bill Withers
Arranged by Carolyn Miller

Accompaniment (Student plays one octave higher than written.)

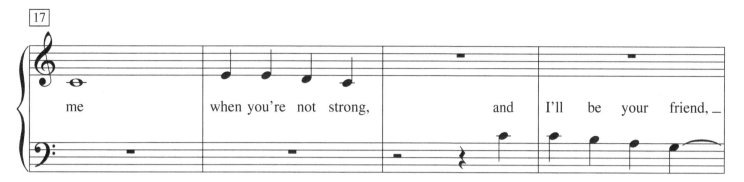

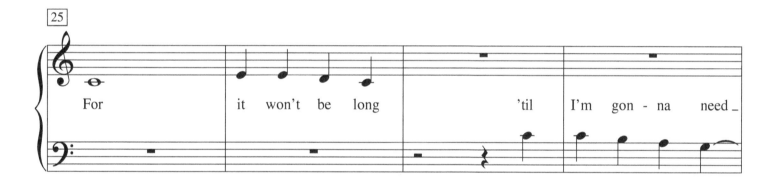

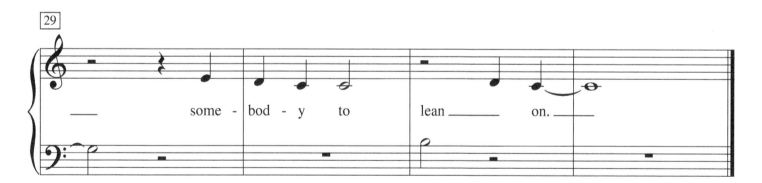

Can You Feel the Love Tonight

from Walt Disney Pictures' THE LION KING

Use after Group II (page 12).

Music by Elton John
Lyrics by Tim Rice
Arranged by Carolyn Miller

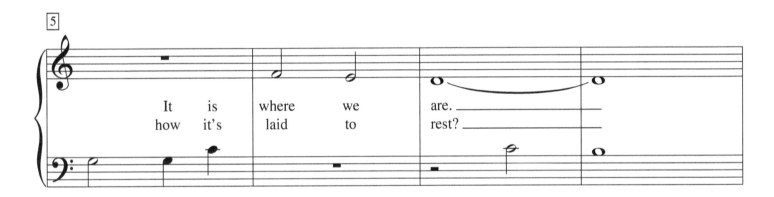

Accompaniment (Student plays one octave higher than written.)

that we got this far. _____ And
lieve the

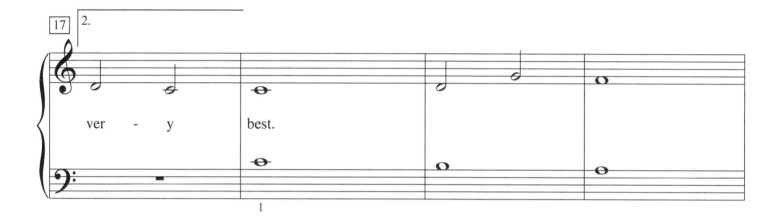

ver - y best.

slower to end

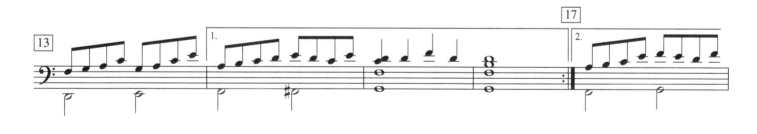

slower to end

Heigh-Ho

Use after Group II (page 12).

Words by Larry Morey
Music by Frank Churchill

Accompaniment (Student plays one octave higher than written.)

ho,   heigh - ho,"   for   if you're feel - ing   low,   you

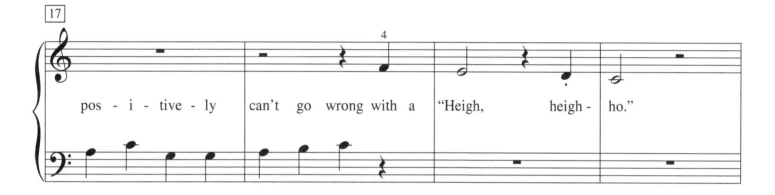

pos - i - tive - ly   can't go wrong with a   "Heigh,   heigh - ho."

8vb

I'm Popeye the Sailor Man

Theme from the Paramount Cartoon POPEYE THE SAILOR

Use after Group III (page 16).

Words and Music by Sammy Lerner
Arranged by Carolyn Miller

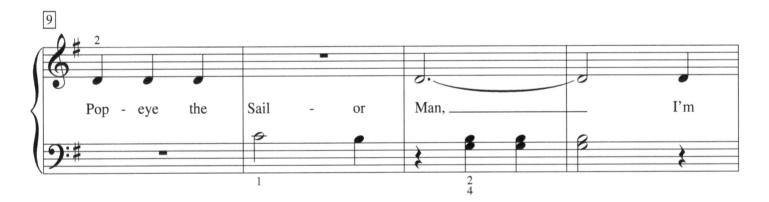

Accompaniment (Student plays one octave higher than written.)

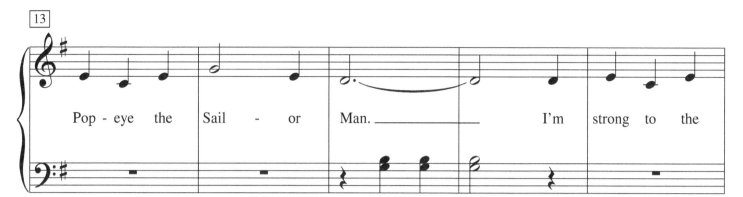

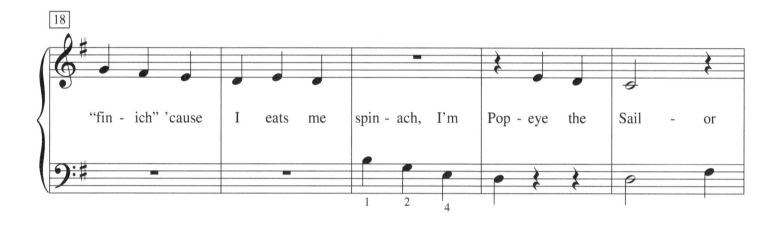

12

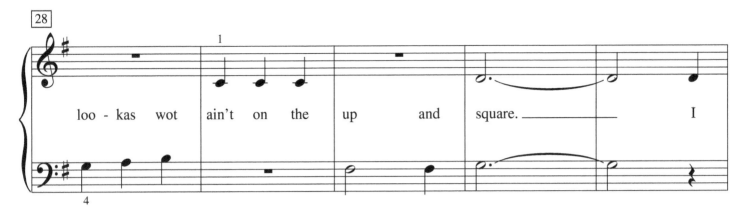

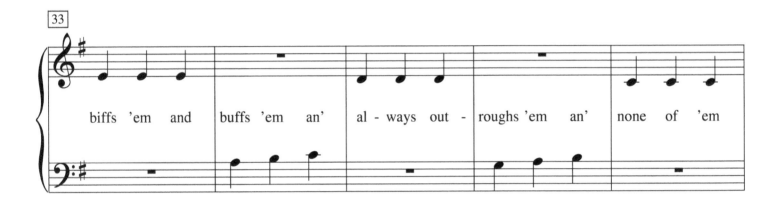

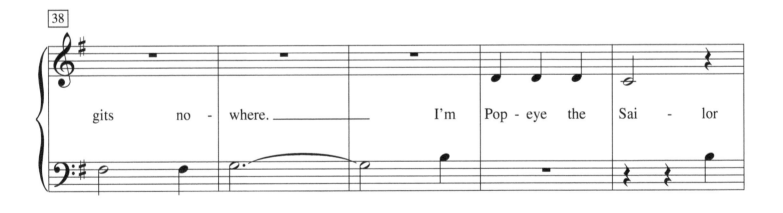

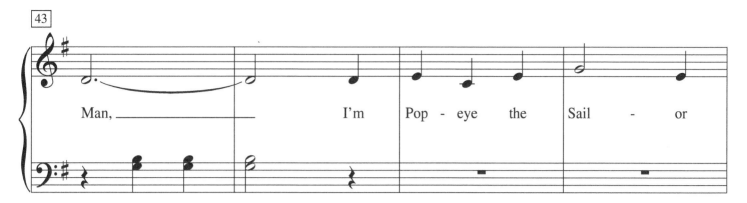

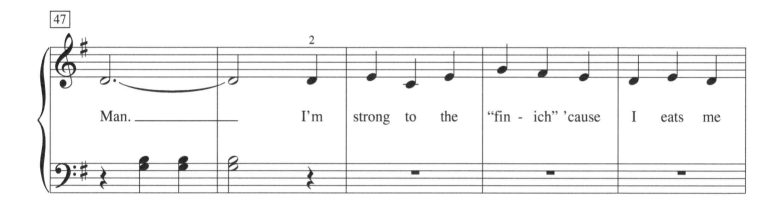

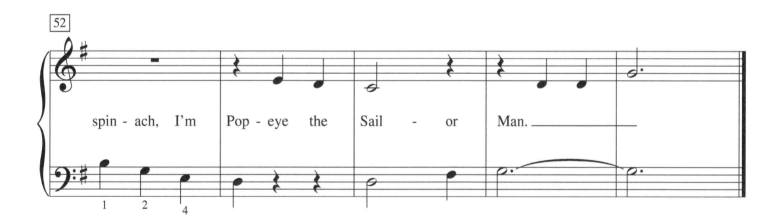

It's a Grand Night for Singing

from STATE FAIR

Use after Group III (page 16).

Lyrics by Oscar Hammerstein II
Music by Richard Rodgers
Arranged by Carolyn Miller

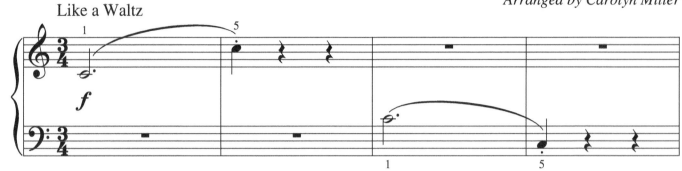

Accompaniment (Student plays one octave higher than written.)

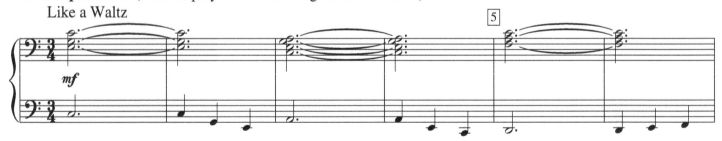

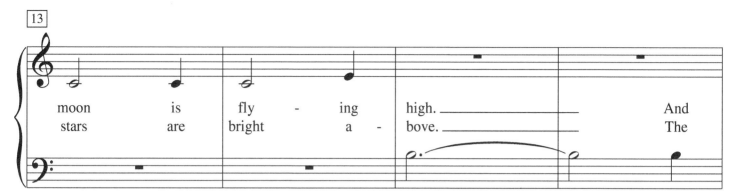

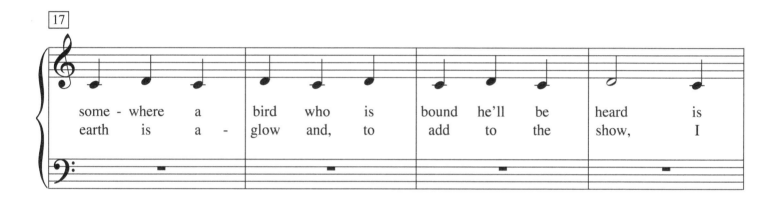

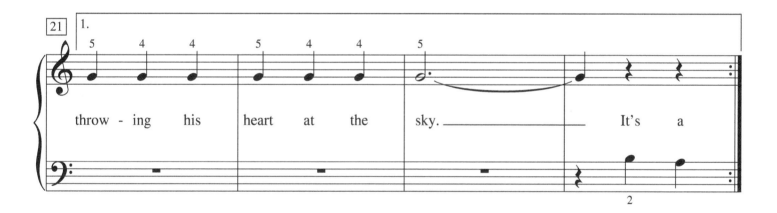

think I am fall - ing in love.

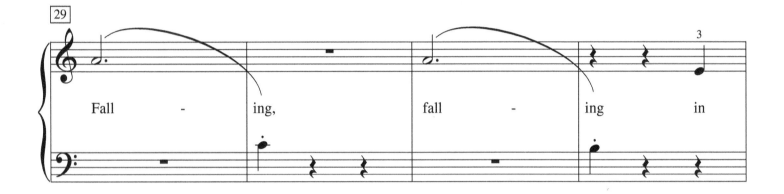

Fall - ing, fall - ing in

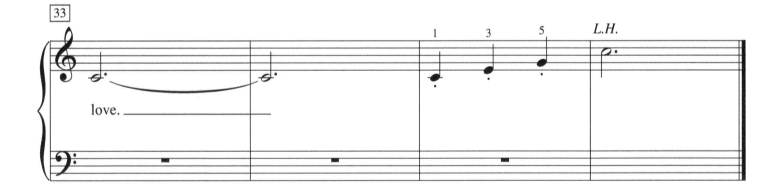

love.

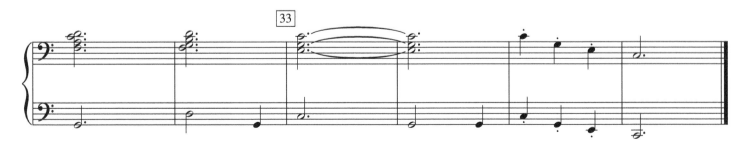

You'll Never Walk Alone

from CAROUSEL

Use after Group IV (page 20).

Lyrics by Oscar Hammerstein II
Music by Richard Rodgers
Arranged by Carolyn Miller

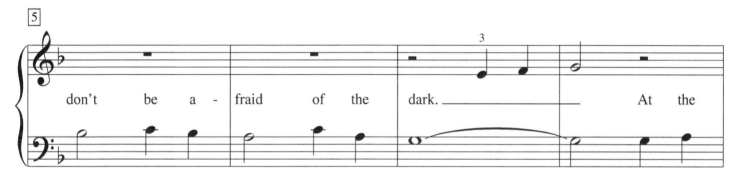

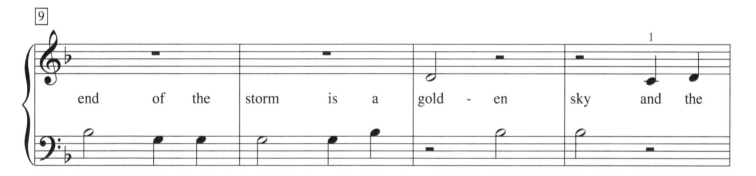

Accompaniment (Student plays one octave higher than written.)

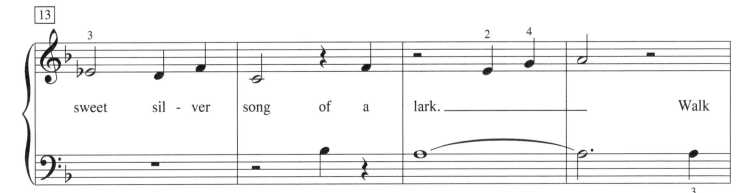

sweet sil - ver song of a lark.＿＿＿＿＿ Walk

on through the wind, walk on through the rain, tho' your

cresc.

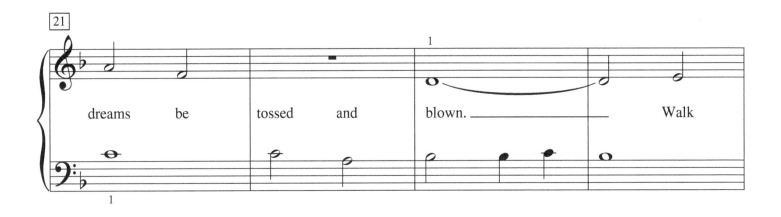

dreams be tossed and blown.＿＿＿＿＿ Walk

cresc.

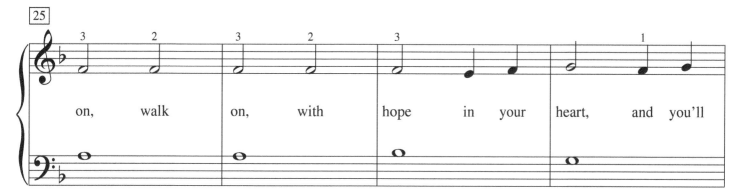

on, walk on, with hope in your heart, and you'll

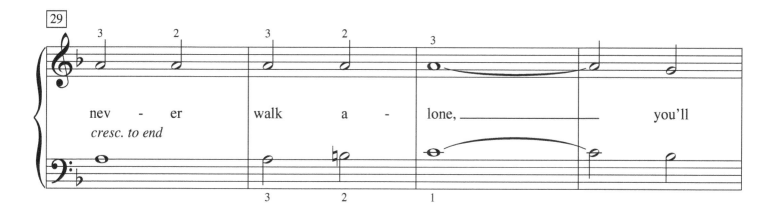

nev - er walk a - lone, you'll

cresc. to end

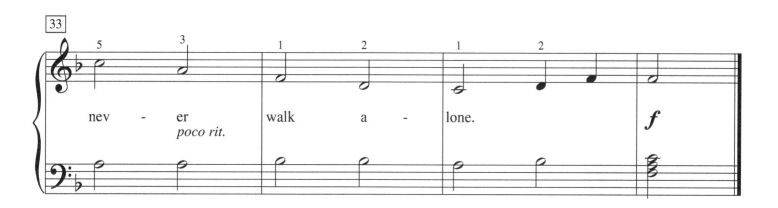

nev - er walk a - lone.

poco rit.

f

cresc. to end

poco rit.

f

A Dream Is a Wish Your Heart Makes

from Walt Disney's CINDERELLA

Use after Group IV (page 20).

Words and Music by Mack David,
Al Hoffman and Jerry Livingston
Arranged by Carolyn Miller

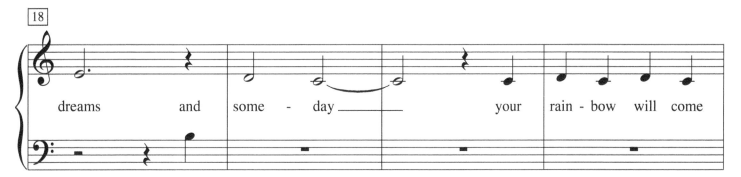

dreams and some - day _____ your rain - bow will come

smil - ing through. No mat - ter how your heart is

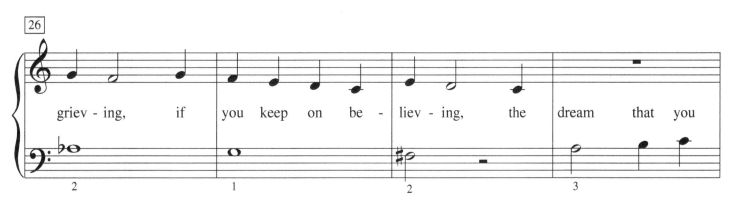

griev - ing, if you keep on be - liev - ing, the dream that you

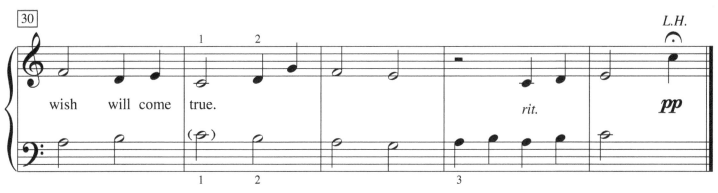

wish will come true. *rit.* *pp*

Any Dream Will Do
from JOSEPH AND THE AMAZING TECHNICOLOR® DREAMCOAT

Use after Group V (page 24).

Music by Andrew Lloyd Webber
Lyrics by Tim Rice
Arranged by Carolyn Miller

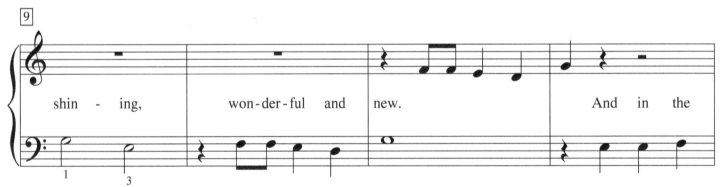

Accompaniment (Student plays one octave higher than written.)

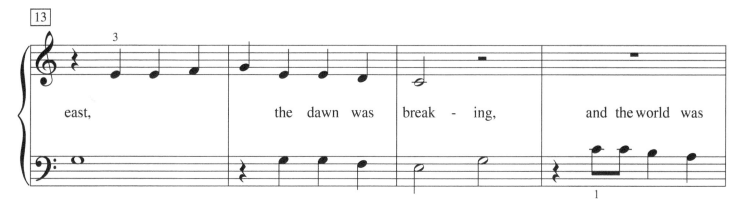

east, the dawn was break - ing, and the world was

wak - ing, an - y dream will do. _____ A

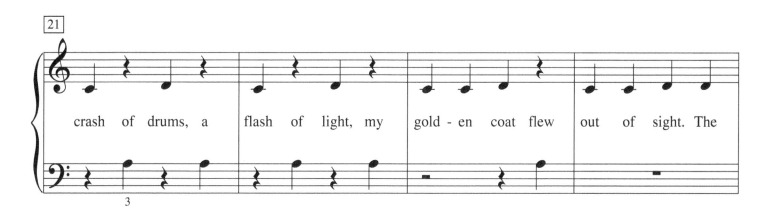

crash of drums, a flash of light, my gold - en coat flew out of sight. The

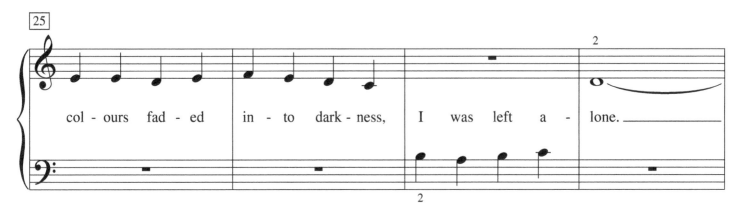

col - ours fad - ed in - to dark - ness, I was left a - lone. _____

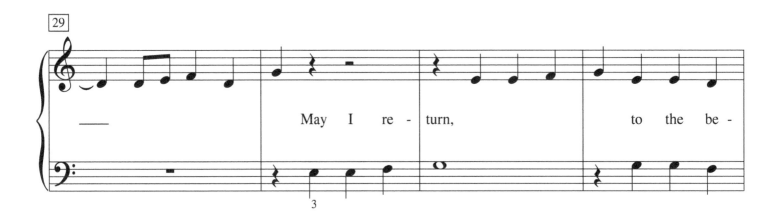

_____ May I re - turn, to the be -

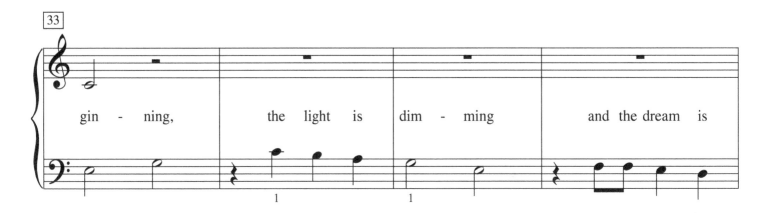

gin - ning, the light is dim - ming and the dream is

too. The world and I, we are still wait - ing,

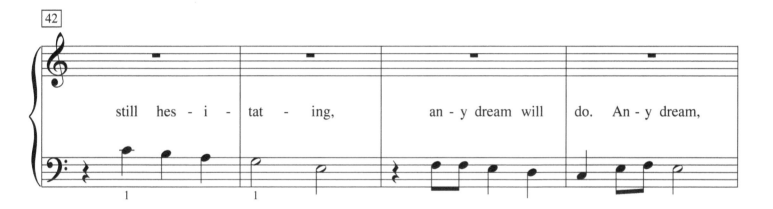

still hes - i - tat - ing, an - y dream will do. An - y dream,

L.H.

an - y dream will, an - y dream, an - y dream will do.

rit.

rit.

So Long, Farewell

from THE SOUND OF MUSIC

Use after Group V (page 24).

Lyrics by Oscar Hammerstein II
Music by Richard Rodgers
Arranged by Carolyn Miller

Steadily, like a clock

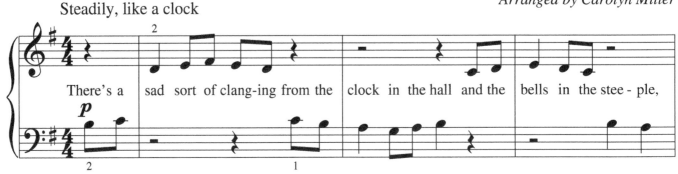

There's a sad sort of clang-ing from the clock in the hall and the bells in the stee - ple,

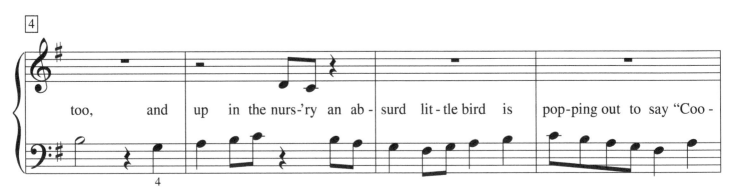

too, and up in the nurs-'ry an ab - surd lit - tle bird is pop-ping out to say "Coo -

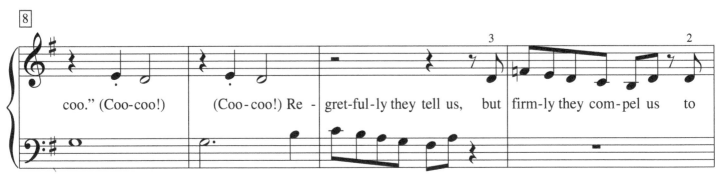

coo." (Coo-coo!) (Coo-coo!) Re - gret-ful-ly they tell us, but firm-ly they com-pel us to

Accompaniment (Student plays one octave higher than written.)

Steadily, like a clock

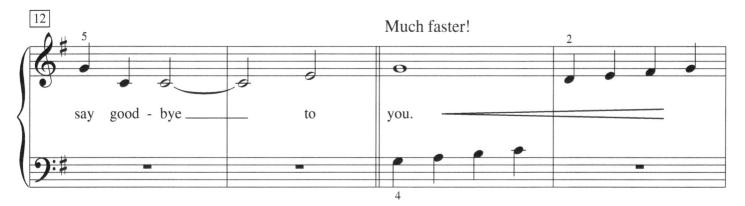

say good - bye _____ to you.

So long, fare - well, Auf

mp

wie - der - sehn, good - night. __ A - dieu, A - dieu, to

Much faster!

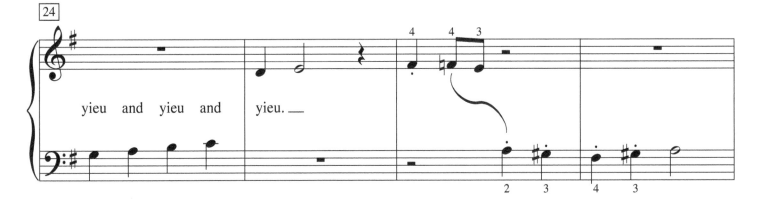

yieu and yieu and yieu. __

So long, fare - well, Auf wie - der - sehn, good -

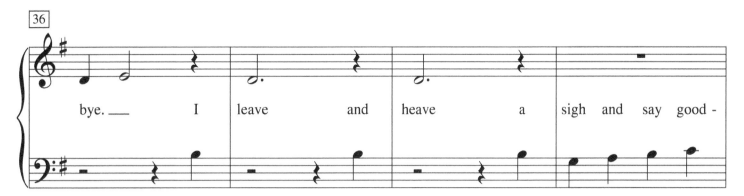

bye. ___ I leave and heave a sigh and say good-

bye. ___ Good - bye, _____ good - bye, _____

___ good - bye, _____ good - bye!

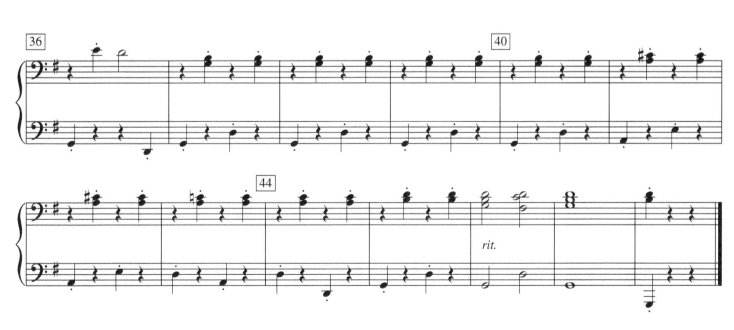

A DOZEN A DAY SONGBOOK SERIES

BROADWAY, MOVIE AND POP HITS

Arranged by Carolyn Miller

The *A Dozen a Day Songbook* series contains wonderful Broadway, movie and pop hits that may be used as companion pieces to the memorable technique exercises in the *A Dozen a Day* series. They are also suitable as supplements for ANY method!

Mini
Early Elementary

A DOZEN A DAY SONGBOOK

Broadway, Movie and Pop Hits
Any Dream Will Do • Can You Feel the Love Tonight • A Dream Is a Wish Your Heart Makes
Heigh-Ho • I'm Popeye the Sailor Man • It's a Grand Night for Singing • Lean on Me
Love Me Tender • So Long, Farewell • You'll Never Walk Alone

THE WILLIS MUSIC COMPANY

MINI
EARLY ELEMENTARY
Songs in the Mini Book:
Any Dream Will Do • Can You Feel the Love Tonight • A Dream Is a Wish Your Heart Makes • Heigh-Ho • I'm Popeye the Sailor Man • It's a Grand Night for Singing • Lean on Me • Love Me Tender • So Long, Farewell • You'll Never Walk Alone.

00416858 Book Only $7.99
00416861 Book/Audio $12.99

PREPARATORY
MID-ELEMENTARY
Songs in the Preparatory Book:
The Bare Necessities • Do-Re-Mi • Getting to Know You • Heart and Soul • Little April Shower • Part of Your World • The Surrey with the Fringe on Top • Swinging on a Star • The Way You Look Tonight • Yellow Submarine.

00416859 Book Only $7.99
00416862 Book/Audio $12.99

BOOK 1
LATER ELEMENTARY
Songs in Book 1:
Cabaret • Climb Ev'ry Mountain • Give a Little Whistle • If I Were a Rich Man • Let It Be • Rock Around the Clock • Twist and Shout • The Wonderful Thing About Tiggers • Yo Ho (A Pirate's Life for Me) • Zip-A-Dee-Doo-Dah.

00416860 Book Only $7.99
00416863 Book/Audio $12.99

BOOK 2
EARLY INTERMEDIATE
Songs in Book 2:
Hallelujah • I Dreamed A Dream • I Walk the Line • I Want to Hold Your Hand • In the Mood • Moon River • Once Upon A Dream • This Land is Your Land • A Whole New World • You Raise Me Up.

00119241 Book Only $6.99
00119242 Book/Audio $12.99

Prices, content, and availability subject to change without notice.

WILLIS MUSIC

EXCLUSIVELY DISTRIBUTED BY
HAL•LEONARD®

www.willispianomusic.com   f   **www.facebook.com/willispianomusic**

0716

A DOZEN A DAY

by Edna Mae Burnam

The **A Dozen A Day** books are universally recognized as one of the most remarkable technique series on the market for all ages! Each book in this series contains short warm-up exercises to be played at the beginning of each practice session, providing excellent day-to-day training for the student. All book/audio versions include orchestrated accompaniments by Ric Ianonne.

MINI BOOK
00404073 Book Only $5.99
00406472 Book/Audio $9.99

PREPARATORY BOOK
00414222 Book Only $5.99
00406476 Book/Audio $9.99

BOOK 1
00413366 Book Only $5.99
00406481 Book/Audio $9.99

BOOK 2
00413826 Book Only $5.99
00406485 Book/Audio $9.99

BOOK 3
00414136 Book Only $6.99
00416760 Book/Audio $10.99

BOOK 4
00415686 Book Only $6.99
00416761 Book/Audio $10.99

**PLAY WITH EASE
IN MANY KEYS**
00416395 Book Only $5.99

**A DOZEN A DAY
ANTHOLOGY**
00158307 Book/Audio $24.99

ALSO AVAILABLE:
The **A Dozen A Day Songbook** series containing Broadway, movie, and pop hits!

Visit Hal Leonard Online at **www.halleonard.com**

WILLIS MUSIC

EXCLUSIVELY DISTRIBUTED BY

HAL•LEONARD®

Prices, contents, and availability subject to change without notice. Prices listed in U.S. funds.